This book belongs to:

____

ISBN: 9798623655059

First Printing, 2020

TakePoint
A scoreboard for winners!
5
17
14
8 2
hello@takepoint.pro | www.takepoint.pro

BACKGAMMON SCORE SHEET

EVENT	ROUND	MATCH LENGTH

GAME			NOTES
1			
2			
3			
4			
5			
6			
7			
8			
9			
10			
11			
12			
13			
14			
15			
16			
17			
18			
19			
20			
21			
22			
23			
24			
25			

BACKGAMMON SCORE SHEET

EVENT	ROUND	MATCH LENGTH

GAME			NOTES
1			
2			
3			
4			
5			
6			
7			
8			
9			
10			
11			
12			
13			
14			
15			
16			
17			
18			
19			
20			
21			
22			
23			
24			
25			

BACKGAMMON SCORE SHEET

EVENT	ROUND	MATCH LENGTH

GAME			NOTES
1			
2			
3			
4			
5			
6			
7			
8			
9			
10			
11			
12			
13			
14			
15			
16			
17			
18			
19			
20			
21			
22			
23			
24			
25			

BACKGAMMON SCORE SHEET

EVENT	ROUND	MATCH LENGTH

GAME			NOTES
1			
2			
3			
4			
5			
6			
7			
8			
9			
10			
11			
12			
13			
14			
15			
16			
17			
18			
19			
20			
21			
22			
23			
24			
25			

BACKGAMMON SCORE SHEET

EVENT	ROUND	MATCH LENGTH

GAME			NOTES
1			
2			
3			
4			
5			
6			
7			
8			
9			
10			
11			
12			
13			
14			
15			
16			
17			
18			
19			
20			
21			
22			
23			
24			
25			

BACKGAMMON SCORE SHEET

EVENT	ROUND	MATCH LENGTH

GAME			NOTES
1			
2			
3			
4			
5			
6			
7			
8			
9			
10			
11			
12			
13			
14			
15			
16			
17			
18			
19			
20			
21			
22			
23			
24			
25			

BACKGAMMON SCORE SHEET

EVENT	ROUND	MATCH LENGTH

GAME			NOTES
1			
2			
3			
4			
5			
6			
7			
8			
9			
10			
11			
12			
13			
14			
15			
16			
17			
18			
19			
20			
21			
22			
23			
24			
25			

BACKGAMMON SCORE SHEET

EVENT	ROUND	MATCH LENGTH

GAME			NOTES
1			
2			
3			
4			
5			
6			
7			
8			
9			
10			
11			
12			
13			
14			
15			
16			
17			
18			
19			
20			
21			
22			
23			
24			
25			

BACKGAMMON SCORE SHEET

EVENT	ROUND	MATCH LENGTH

GAME			NOTES
1			
2			
3			
4			
5			
6			
7			
8			
9			
10			
11			
12			
13			
14			
15			
16			
17			
18			
19			
20			
21			
22			
23			
24			
25			

BACKGAMMON SCORE SHEET

EVENT	ROUND	MATCH LENGTH

GAME			NOTES
1			
2			
3			
4			
5			
6			
7			
8			
9			
10			
11			
12			
13			
14			
15			
16			
17			
18			
19			
20			
21			
22			
23			
24			
25			

BACKGAMMON SCORE SHEET

EVENT	ROUND	MATCH LENGTH

GAME			NOTES
1			
2			
3			
4			
5			
6			
7			
8			
9			
10			
11			
12			
13			
14			
15			
16			
17			
18			
19			
20			
21			
22			
23			
24			
25			

BACKGAMMON SCORE SHEET

EVENT	ROUND	MATCH LENGTH

GAME			NOTES
1			
2			
3			
4			
5			
6			
7			
8			
9			
10			
11			
12			
13			
14			
15			
16			
17			
18			
19			
20			
21			
22			
23			
24			
25			

BACKGAMMON SCORE SHEET

EVENT	ROUND	MATCH LENGTH

GAME			NOTES
1			
2			
3			
4			
5			
6			
7			
8			
9			
10			
11			
12			
13			
14			
15			
16			
17			
18			
19			
20			
21			
22			
23			
24			
25			

BACKGAMMON SCORE SHEET

EVENT	ROUND	MATCH LENGTH

GAME			NOTES
1			
2			
3			
4			
5			
6			
7			
8			
9			
10			
11			
12			
13			
14			
15			
16			
17			
18			
19			
20			
21			
22			
23			
24			
25			

BACKGAMMON SCORE SHEET

EVENT	ROUND	MATCH LENGTH

GAME			NOTES
1			
2			
3			
4			
5			
6			
7			
8			
9			
10			
11			
12			
13			
14			
15			
16			
17			
18			
19			
20			
21			
22			
23			
24			
25			

BACKGAMMON SCORE SHEET

EVENT	ROUND	MATCH LENGTH

GAME			NOTES
1			
2			
3			
4			
5			
6			
7			
8			
9			
10			
11			
12			
13			
14			
15			
16			
17			
18			
19			
20			
21			
22			
23			
24			
25			

BACKGAMMON SCORE SHEET

EVENT	ROUND	MATCH LENGTH

GAME			NOTES
1			
2			
3			
4			
5			
6			
7			
8			
9			
10			
11			
12			
13			
14			
15			
16			
17			
18			
19			
20			
21			
22			
23			
24			
25			

BACKGAMMON SCORE SHEET

EVENT	ROUND	MATCH LENGTH

GAME			NOTES
1			
2			
3			
4			
5			
6			
7			
8			
9			
10			
11			
12			
13			
14			
15			
16			
17			
18			
19			
20			
21			
22			
23			
24			
25			

BACKGAMMON SCORE SHEET

EVENT	ROUND	MATCH LENGTH

GAME			NOTES
1			
2			
3			
4			
5			
6			
7			
8			
9			
10			
11			
12			
13			
14			
15			
16			
17			
18			
19			
20			
21			
22			
23			
24			
25			

BACKGAMMON SCORE SHEET

EVENT	ROUND	MATCH LENGTH

GAME			NOTES
1			
2			
3			
4			
5			
6			
7			
8			
9			
10			
11			
12			
13			
14			
15			
16			
17			
18			
19			
20			
21			
22			
23			
24			
25			

BACKGAMMON SCORE SHEET

EVENT	ROUND	MATCH LENGTH

GAME			NOTES
1			
2			
3			
4			
5			
6			
7			
8			
9			
10			
11			
12			
13			
14			
15			
16			
17			
18			
19			
20			
21			
22			
23			
24			
25			

BACKGAMMON SCORE SHEET

EVENT

ROUND

MATCH LENGTH

GAME			NOTES
1			
2			
3			
4			
5			
6			
7			
8			
9			
10			
11			
12			
13			
14			
15			
16			
17			
18			
19			
20			
21			
22			
23			
24			
25			

BACKGAMMON SCORE SHEET

EVENT	ROUND	MATCH LENGTH

GAME			NOTES
1			
2			
3			
4			
5			
6			
7			
8			
9			
10			
11			
12			
13			
14			
15			
16			
17			
18			
19			
20			
21			
22			
23			
24			
25			

BACKGAMMON SCORE SHEET

EVENT	ROUND	MATCH LENGTH

GAME			NOTES
1			
2			
3			
4			
5			
6			
7			
8			
9			
10			
11			
12			
13			
14			
15			
16			
17			
18			
19			
20			
21			
22			
23			
24			
25			

BACKGAMMON SCORE SHEET

EVENT	ROUND	MATCH LENGTH

GAME			NOTES
1			
2			
3			
4			
5			
6			
7			
8			
9			
10			
11			
12			
13			
14			
15			
16			
17			
18			
19			
20			
21			
22			
23			
24			
25			

BACKGAMMON SCORE SHEET

EVENT	ROUND	MATCH LENGTH

GAME			NOTES
1			
2			
3			
4			
5			
6			
7			
8			
9			
10			
11			
12			
13			
14			
15			
16			
17			
18			
19			
20			
21			
22			
23			
24			
25			

BACKGAMMON SCORE SHEET

EVENT	ROUND	MATCH LENGTH

GAME			NOTES
1			
2			
3			
4			
5			
6			
7			
8			
9			
10			
11			
12			
13			
14			
15			
16			
17			
18			
19			
20			
21			
22			
23			
24			
25			

BACKGAMMON SCORE SHEET

EVENT	ROUND	MATCH LENGTH

GAME			NOTES
1			
2			
3			
4			
5			
6			
7			
8			
9			
10			
11			
12			
13			
14			
15			
16			
17			
18			
19			
20			
21			
22			
23			
24			
25			

BACKGAMMON SCORE SHEET

EVENT	ROUND	MATCH LENGTH

GAME			NOTES
1			
2			
3			
4			
5			
6			
7			
8			
9			
10			
11			
12			
13			
14			
15			
16			
17			
18			
19			
20			
21			
22			
23			
24			
25			

BACKGAMMON SCORE SHEET

EVENT	ROUND	MATCH LENGTH

GAME			NOTES
1			
2			
3			
4			
5			
6			
7			
8			
9			
10			
11			
12			
13			
14			
15			
16			
17			
18			
19			
20			
21			
22			
23			
24			
25			

BACKGAMMON SCORE SHEET

EVENT	ROUND	MATCH LENGTH

GAME			NOTES
1			
2			
3			
4			
5			
6			
7			
8			
9			
10			
11			
12			
13			
14			
15			
16			
17			
18			
19			
20			
21			
22			
23			
24			
25			

BACKGAMMON SCORE SHEET

EVENT

ROUND

MATCH LENGTH

GAME			NOTES
1			
2			
3			
4			
5			
6			
7			
8			
9			
10			
11			
12			
13			
14			
15			
16			
17			
18			
19			
20			
21			
22			
23			
24			
25			

BACKGAMMON SCORE SHEET

EVENT	ROUND	MATCH LENGTH

GAME			NOTES
1			
2			
3			
4			
5			
6			
7			
8			
9			
10			
11			
12			
13			
14			
15			
16			
17			
18			
19			
20			
21			
22			
23			
24			
25			

BACKGAMMON SCORE SHEET

EVENT	ROUND	MATCH LENGTH

GAME			NOTES
1			
2			
3			
4			
5			
6			
7			
8			
9			
10			
11			
12			
13			
14			
15			
16			
17			
18			
19			
20			
21			
22			
23			
24			
25			

BACKGAMMON SCORE SHEET

EVENT	ROUND	MATCH LENGTH

GAME			NOTES
1			
2			
3			
4			
5			
6			
7			
8			
9			
10			
11			
12			
13			
14			
15			
16			
17			
18			
19			
20			
21			
22			
23			
24			
25			

BACKGAMMON SCORE SHEET

EVENT	ROUND	MATCH LENGTH

GAME			NOTES
1			
2			
3			
4			
5			
6			
7			
8			
9			
10			
11			
12			
13			
14			
15			
16			
17			
18			
19			
20			
21			
22			
23			
24			
25			

BACKGAMMON SCORE SHEET

EVENT	ROUND	MATCH LENGTH

GAME			NOTES
1			
2			
3			
4			
5			
6			
7			
8			
9			
10			
11			
12			
13			
14			
15			
16			
17			
18			
19			
20			
21			
22			
23			
24			
25			

BACKGAMMON SCORE SHEET

EVENT	ROUND	MATCH LENGTH

GAME			NOTES
1			
2			
3			
4			
5			
6			
7			
8			
9			
10			
11			
12			
13			
14			
15			
16			
17			
18			
19			
20			
21			
22			
23			
24			
25			

BACKGAMMON SCORE SHEET

EVENT	ROUND	MATCH LENGTH

GAME			NOTES
1			
2			
3			
4			
5			
6			
7			
8			
9			
10			
11			
12			
13			
14			
15			
16			
17			
18			
19			
20			
21			
22			
23			
24			
25			

BACKGAMMON SCORE SHEET

EVENT	ROUND	MATCH LENGTH

GAME			NOTES
1			
2			
3			
4			
5			
6			
7			
8			
9			
10			
11			
12			
13			
14			
15			
16			
17			
18			
19			
20			
21			
22			
23			
24			
25			

BACKGAMMON SCORE SHEET

EVENT	ROUND	MATCH LENGTH

GAME			NOTES
1			
2			
3			
4			
5			
6			
7			
8			
9			
10			
11			
12			
13			
14			
15			
16			
17			
18			
19			
20			
21			
22			
23			
24			
25			

BACKGAMMON SCORE SHEET

EVENT

ROUND

MATCH LENGTH

GAME			NOTES
1			
2			
3			
4			
5			
6			
7			
8			
9			
10			
11			
12			
13			
14			
15			
16			
17			
18			
19			
20			
21			
22			
23			
24			
25			

BACKGAMMON SCORE SHEET

EVENT	ROUND	MATCH LENGTH

GAME			NOTES
1			
2			
3			
4			
5			
6			
7			
8			
9			
10			
11			
12			
13			
14			
15			
16			
17			
18			
19			
20			
21			
22			
23			
24			
25			

BACKGAMMON SCORE SHEET

EVENT	ROUND	MATCH LENGTH

GAME			NOTES
1			
2			
3			
4			
5			
6			
7			
8			
9			
10			
11			
12			
13			
14			
15			
16			
17			
18			
19			
20			
21			
22			
23			
24			
25			

BACKGAMMON SCORE SHEET

EVENT	ROUND	MATCH LENGTH

GAME			NOTES
1			
2			
3			
4			
5			
6			
7			
8			
9			
10			
11			
12			
13			
14			
15			
16			
17			
18			
19			
20			
21			
22			
23			
24			
25			

BACKGAMMON SCORE SHEET

EVENT	ROUND	MATCH LENGTH

GAME			NOTES
1			
2			
3			
4			
5			
6			
7			
8			
9			
10			
11			
12			
13			
14			
15			
16			
17			
18			
19			
20			
21			
22			
23			
24			
25			

BACKGAMMON SCORE SHEET

EVENT	ROUND	MATCH LENGTH

GAME			NOTES
1			
2			
3			
4			
5			
6			
7			
8			
9			
10			
11			
12			
13			
14			
15			
16			
17			
18			
19			
20			
21			
22			
23			
24			
25			

BACKGAMMON SCORE SHEET

EVENT	ROUND	MATCH LENGTH

GAME			NOTES
1			
2			
3			
4			
5			
6			
7			
8			
9			
10			
11			
12			
13			
14			
15			
16			
17			
18			
19			
20			
21			
22			
23			
24			
25			

BACKGAMMON SCORE SHEET

EVENT	ROUND	MATCH LENGTH

GAME			NOTES
1			
2			
3			
4			
5			
6			
7			
8			
9			
10			
11			
12			
13			
14			
15			
16			
17			
18			
19			
20			
21			
22			
23			
24			
25			

BACKGAMMON SCORE SHEET

EVENT	ROUND	MATCH LENGTH

GAME			NOTES
1			
2			
3			
4			
5			
6			
7			
8			
9			
10			
11			
12			
13			
14			
15			
16			
17			
18			
19			
20			
21			
22			
23			
24			
25			

BACKGAMMON SCORE SHEET

EVENT	ROUND	MATCH LENGTH

GAME			NOTES
1			
2			
3			
4			
5			
6			
7			
8			
9			
10			
11			
12			
13			
14			
15			
16			
17			
18			
19			
20			
21			
22			
23			
24			
25			

BACKGAMMON SCORE SHEET

EVENT	ROUND	MATCH LENGTH

GAME			NOTES
1			
2			
3			
4			
5			
6			
7			
8			
9			
10			
11			
12			
13			
14			
15			
16			
17			
18			
19			
20			
21			
22			
23			
24			
25			

BACKGAMMON SCORE SHEET

EVENT	ROUND	MATCH LENGTH

GAME			NOTES
1			
2			
3			
4			
5			
6			
7			
8			
9			
10			
11			
12			
13			
14			
15			
16			
17			
18			
19			
20			
21			
22			
23			
24			
25			

BACKGAMMON SCORE SHEET

EVENT	ROUND	MATCH LENGTH

GAME			NOTES
1			
2			
3			
4			
5			
6			
7			
8			
9			
10			
11			
12			
13			
14			
15			
16			
17			
18			
19			
20			
21			
22			
23			
24			
25			

BACKGAMMON SCORE SHEET

EVENT	ROUND	MATCH LENGTH

GAME			NOTES
1			
2			
3			
4			
5			
6			
7			
8			
9			
10			
11			
12			
13			
14			
15			
16			
17			
18			
19			
20			
21			
22			
23			
24			
25			

BACKGAMMON SCORE SHEET

EVENT	ROUND	MATCH LENGTH

GAME			NOTES
1			
2			
3			
4			
5			
6			
7			
8			
9			
10			
11			
12			
13			
14			
15			
16			
17			
18			
19			
20			
21			
22			
23			
24			
25			

BACKGAMMON SCORE SHEET

EVENT	ROUND	MATCH LENGTH

GAME			NOTES
1			
2			
3			
4			
5			
6			
7			
8			
9			
10			
11			
12			
13			
14			
15			
16			
17			
18			
19			
20			
21			
22			
23			
24			
25			

BACKGAMMON SCORE SHEET

EVENT	ROUND	MATCH LENGTH

GAME			NOTES
1			
2			
3			
4			
5			
6			
7			
8			
9			
10			
11			
12			
13			
14			
15			
16			
17			
18			
19			
20			
21			
22			
23			
24			
25			

BACKGAMMON SCORE SHEET

EVENT	ROUND	MATCH LENGTH

GAME			NOTES
1			
2			
3			
4			
5			
6			
7			
8			
9			
10			
11			
12			
13			
14			
15			
16			
17			
18			
19			
20			
21			
22			
23			
24			
25			

BACKGAMMON SCORE SHEET

EVENT	ROUND	MATCH LENGTH

GAME			NOTES
1			
2			
3			
4			
5			
6			
7			
8			
9			
10			
11			
12			
13			
14			
15			
16			
17			
18			
19			
20			
21			
22			
23			
24			
25			

BACKGAMMON SCORE SHEET

EVENT	ROUND	MATCH LENGTH

GAME			NOTES
1			
2			
3			
4			
5			
6			
7			
8			
9			
10			
11			
12			
13			
14			
15			
16			
17			
18			
19			
20			
21			
22			
23			
24			
25			

BACKGAMMON SCORE SHEET

EVENT	ROUND	MATCH LENGTH

GAME			NOTES
1			
2			
3			
4			
5			
6			
7			
8			
9			
10			
11			
12			
13			
14			
15			
16			
17			
18			
19			
20			
21			
22			
23			
24			
25			

BACKGAMMON SCORE SHEET

EVENT	ROUND	MATCH LENGTH

GAME			NOTES
1			
2			
3			
4			
5			
6			
7			
8			
9			
10			
11			
12			
13			
14			
15			
16			
17			
18			
19			
20			
21			
22			
23			
24			
25			

BACKGAMMON SCORE SHEET

EVENT

ROUND

MATCH LENGTH

GAME			NOTES
1			
2			
3			
4			
5			
6			
7			
8			
9			
10			
11			
12			
13			
14			
15			
16			
17			
18			
19			
20			
21			
22			
23			
24			
25			

BACKGAMMON SCORE SHEET

EVENT	ROUND	MATCH LENGTH

GAME			NOTES
1			
2			
3			
4			
5			
6			
7			
8			
9			
10			
11			
12			
13			
14			
15			
16			
17			
18			
19			
20			
21			
22			
23			
24			
25			

BACKGAMMON SCORE SHEET

EVENT	ROUND	MATCH LENGTH

GAME			NOTES
1			
2			
3			
4			
5			
6			
7			
8			
9			
10			
11			
12			
13			
14			
15			
16			
17			
18			
19			
20			
21			
22			
23			
24			
25			

BACKGAMMON SCORE SHEET

EVENT	ROUND	MATCH LENGTH

GAME			NOTES
1			
2			
3			
4			
5			
6			
7			
8			
9			
10			
11			
12			
13			
14			
15			
16			
17			
18			
19			
20			
21			
22			
23			
24			
25			

BACKGAMMON SCORE SHEET

EVENT	ROUND	MATCH LENGTH

GAME			NOTES
1			
2			
3			
4			
5			
6			
7			
8			
9			
10			
11			
12			
13			
14			
15			
16			
17			
18			
19			
20			
21			
22			
23			
24			
25			

BACKGAMMON SCORE SHEET

EVENT	ROUND	MATCH LENGTH

GAME			NOTES
1			
2			
3			
4			
5			
6			
7			
8			
9			
10			
11			
12			
13			
14			
15			
16			
17			
18			
19			
20			
21			
22			
23			
24			
25			

BACKGAMMON SCORE SHEET

EVENT	ROUND	MATCH LENGTH

GAME			NOTES
1			
2			
3			
4			
5			
6			
7			
8			
9			
10			
11			
12			
13			
14			
15			
16			
17			
18			
19			
20			
21			
22			
23			
24			
25			

BACKGAMMON SCORE SHEET

EVENT	ROUND	MATCH LENGTH

GAME			NOTES
1			
2			
3			
4			
5			
6			
7			
8			
9			
10			
11			
12			
13			
14			
15			
16			
17			
18			
19			
20			
21			
22			
23			
24			
25			

BACKGAMMON SCORE SHEET

EVENT	ROUND	MATCH LENGTH

GAME			NOTES
1			
2			
3			
4			
5			
6			
7			
8			
9			
10			
11			
12			
13			
14			
15			
16			
17			
18			
19			
20			
21			
22			
23			
24			
25			

BACKGAMMON SCORE SHEET

EVENT	ROUND	MATCH LENGTH

GAME			NOTES
1			
2			
3			
4			
5			
6			
7			
8			
9			
10			
11			
12			
13			
14			
15			
16			
17			
18			
19			
20			
21			
22			
23			
24			
25			

BACKGAMMON SCORE SHEET

EVENT	ROUND	MATCH LENGTH

GAME			NOTES
1			
2			
3			
4			
5			
6			
7			
8			
9			
10			
11			
12			
13			
14			
15			
16			
17			
18			
19			
20			
21			
22			
23			
24			
25			

BACKGAMMON SCORE SHEET

EVENT	ROUND	MATCH LENGTH

GAME			NOTES
1			
2			
3			
4			
5			
6			
7			
8			
9			
10			
11			
12			
13			
14			
15			
16			
17			
18			
19			
20			
21			
22			
23			
24			
25			

BACKGAMMON SCORE SHEET

EVENT	ROUND	MATCH LENGTH

GAME			NOTES
1			
2			
3			
4			
5			
6			
7			
8			
9			
10			
11			
12			
13			
14			
15			
16			
17			
18			
19			
20			
21			
22			
23			
24			
25			

BACKGAMMON SCORE SHEET

EVENT	ROUND	MATCH LENGTH

GAME			NOTES
1			
2			
3			
4			
5			
6			
7			
8			
9			
10			
11			
12			
13			
14			
15			
16			
17			
18			
19			
20			
21			
22			
23			
24			
25			

BACKGAMMON SCORE SHEET

EVENT	ROUND	MATCH LENGTH

GAME			NOTES
1			
2			
3			
4			
5			
6			
7			
8			
9			
10			
11			
12			
13			
14			
15			
16			
17			
18			
19			
20			
21			
22			
23			
24			
25			

BACKGAMMON SCORE SHEET

EVENT	ROUND	MATCH LENGTH

GAME			NOTES
1			
2			
3			
4			
5			
6			
7			
8			
9			
10			
11			
12			
13			
14			
15			
16			
17			
18			
19			
20			
21			
22			
23			
24			
25			

BACKGAMMON SCORE SHEET

EVENT	ROUND	MATCH LENGTH

GAME			NOTES
1			
2			
3			
4			
5			
6			
7			
8			
9			
10			
11			
12			
13			
14			
15			
16			
17			
18			
19			
20			
21			
22			
23			
24			
25			

BACKGAMMON SCORE SHEET

EVENT	ROUND	MATCH LENGTH

GAME			NOTES
1			
2			
3			
4			
5			
6			
7			
8			
9			
10			
11			
12			
13			
14			
15			
16			
17			
18			
19			
20			
21			
22			
23			
24			
25			

BACKGAMMON SCORE SHEET

EVENT	ROUND	MATCH LENGTH

GAME			NOTES
1			
2			
3			
4			
5			
6			
7			
8			
9			
10			
11			
12			
13			
14			
15			
16			
17			
18			
19			
20			
21			
22			
23			
24			
25			

BACKGAMMON SCORE SHEET

EVENT	ROUND	MATCH LENGTH

GAME			NOTES
1			
2			
3			
4			
5			
6			
7			
8			
9			
10			
11			
12			
13			
14			
15			
16			
17			
18			
19			
20			
21			
22			
23			
24			
25			

BACKGAMMON SCORE SHEET

EVENT	ROUND	MATCH LENGTH

GAME			NOTES
1			
2			
3			
4			
5			
6			
7			
8			
9			
10			
11			
12			
13			
14			
15			
16			
17			
18			
19			
20			
21			
22			
23			
24			
25			

BACKGAMMON SCORE SHEET

EVENT	ROUND	MATCH LENGTH

GAME			NOTES
1			
2			
3			
4			
5			
6			
7			
8			
9			
10			
11			
12			
13			
14			
15			
16			
17			
18			
19			
20			
21			
22			
23			
24			
25			

BACKGAMMON SCORE SHEET

EVENT	ROUND	MATCH LENGTH

GAME			NOTES
1			
2			
3			
4			
5			
6			
7			
8			
9			
10			
11			
12			
13			
14			
15			
16			
17			
18			
19			
20			
21			
22			
23			
24			
25			

BACKGAMMON SCORE SHEET

EVENT	ROUND	MATCH LENGTH

GAME			NOTES
1			
2			
3			
4			
5			
6			
7			
8			
9			
10			
11			
12			
13			
14			
15			
16			
17			
18			
19			
20			
21			
22			
23			
24			
25			

BACKGAMMON SCORE SHEET

EVENT	ROUND	MATCH LENGTH

GAME			NOTES
1			
2			
3			
4			
5			
6			
7			
8			
9			
10			
11			
12			
13			
14			
15			
16			
17			
18			
19			
20			
21			
22			
23			
24			
25			

BACKGAMMON SCORE SHEET

EVENT	ROUND	MATCH LENGTH

GAME			NOTES
1			
2			
3			
4			
5			
6			
7			
8			
9			
10			
11			
12			
13			
14			
15			
16			
17			
18			
19			
20			
21			
22			
23			
24			
25			

BACKGAMMON SCORE SHEET

EVENT	ROUND	MATCH LENGTH

GAME			NOTES
1			
2			
3			
4			
5			
6			
7			
8			
9			
10			
11			
12			
13			
14			
15			
16			
17			
18			
19			
20			
21			
22			
23			
24			
25			

BACKGAMMON SCORE SHEET

EVENT	ROUND	MATCH LENGTH

GAME			NOTES
1			
2			
3			
4			
5			
6			
7			
8			
9			
10			
11			
12			
13			
14			
15			
16			
17			
18			
19			
20			
21			
22			
23			
24			
25			

BACKGAMMON SCORE SHEET

EVENT	ROUND	MATCH LENGTH

GAME			NOTES
1			
2			
3			
4			
5			
6			
7			
8			
9			
10			
11			
12			
13			
14			
15			
16			
17			
18			
19			
20			
21			
22			
23			
24			
25			

BACKGAMMON SCORE SHEET

EVENT	ROUND	MATCH LENGTH

GAME			NOTES
1			
2			
3			
4			
5			
6			
7			
8			
9			
10			
11			
12			
13			
14			
15			
16			
17			
18			
19			
20			
21			
22			
23			
24			
25			

BACKGAMMON SCORE SHEET

EVENT	ROUND	MATCH LENGTH

GAME			NOTES
1			
2			
3			
4			
5			
6			
7			
8			
9			
10			
11			
12			
13			
14			
15			
16			
17			
18			
19			
20			
21			
22			
23			
24			
25			

BACKGAMMON SCORE SHEET

EVENT	ROUND	MATCH LENGTH

GAME			NOTES
1			
2			
3			
4			
5			
6			
7			
8			
9			
10			
11			
12			
13			
14			
15			
16			
17			
18			
19			
20			
21			
22			
23			
24			
25			

BACKGAMMON SCORE SHEET

EVENT	ROUND	MATCH LENGTH

GAME			NOTES
1			
2			
3			
4			
5			
6			
7			
8			
9			
10			
11			
12			
13			
14			
15			
16			
17			
18			
19			
20			
21			
22			
23			
24			
25			

BACKGAMMON SCORE SHEET

EVENT	ROUND	MATCH LENGTH

GAME			NOTES
1			
2			
3			
4			
5			
6			
7			
8			
9			
10			
11			
12			
13			
14			
15			
16			
17			
18			
19			
20			
21			
22			
23			
24			
25			

BACKGAMMON SCORE SHEET

EVENT	ROUND	MATCH LENGTH

GAME			NOTES
1			
2			
3			
4			
5			
6			
7			
8			
9			
10			
11			
12			
13			
14			
15			
16			
17			
18			
19			
20			
21			
22			
23			
24			
25			

BACKGAMMON SCORE SHEET

EVENT	ROUND	MATCH LENGTH

GAME			NOTES
1			
2			
3			
4			
5			
6			
7			
8			
9			
10			
11			
12			
13			
14			
15			
16			
17			
18			
19			
20			
21			
22			
23			
24			
25			

BACKGAMMON SCORE SHEET

EVENT	ROUND	MATCH LENGTH

GAME			NOTES
1			
2			
3			
4			
5			
6			
7			
8			
9			
10			
11			
12			
13			
14			
15			
16			
17			
18			
19			
20			
21			
22			
23			
24			
25			

Made in the USA
Monee, IL
10 December 2022

20768477R00057